Sarah's
Journey of Faith

Volume 1:

Life and Conversion—
A Thirty-Day Devotional

Sarah Liu

WESTBOW·
P R E S S
A DIVISION OF THOMAS NELSON
& ZONDERVAN

The Scripture quotations are taken from the New International
Version © 1984 by the International Bible Society.

WestBow Press books may be ordered through
booksellers or by contacting:

WestBow Press
A Division of Thomas Nelson & Zondervan
1663 Liberty Drive
Bloomington, IN 47403
www.westbowpress.com
1 (866) 928-1240

ISBN: 978-1-4908-2619-6 (sc)
ISBN: 978-1-4908-2621-9 (hc)
ISBN: 978-1-4908-2620-2 (e)

Library of Congress Control Number: 2014902745

Printed in the United States of America.

WestBow Press rev. date: 03/18/2014

Contents

To my sisters and brothers around the world who are still suffering for Christ— theirs is the better resurrection!

"Others were tortured and refused to be released, so that they might gain a better resurrection."

—Hebrews 11:35c

Preface

"Do you have a book?" This question often follows me wherever I speak. My answer is, "No, I do not have anything published." I see disappointment on their faces, and I am saddened. They often say things like, "I want to share your story with my church [or pastor or friend]." And I think that another opportunity to tell the story of God's marvelous work in the life of the believer, persecuted or not, has been missed.

I believe that Satan has two primary ways of silencing believers. The first way is to intimidate them into silence by censorship to persecution, and the second is to seduce them out of Christ's way. Fear and pleasure become powerful temptations away from the Lord if we are not on guard.

In China, Satan uses fear, but in America, he uses pleasure. Either way, the diabolical goal is the same … silence!

I choose not to be silent, and I know neither do you. That's why this particular devotional will be helpful. Together, as we travel this journey of faith, we will both be made stronger and emboldened to speak the Word of God as we should.

Sarah Liu
Los Angeles, California
October 2012

Introduction

This book is not intended to be a formal theological text. Rather, it reflects my personal life experiences in China and my relationship with God. I am not writing as an expert but as an ordinary woman, telling stories about her walk with God. There's nothing worth saying, apart from my relationship with God. This first volume recalls my early story before I was a believer. Yet my reflection on these stories reveals God's work in covering me with his grace long before I even knew him. God was with me; I was not with God. He selected me and was already working in my life.

Chairman Mao, then chairman of the Communist Party of China, passed away in 1976, when I was about five years old. I didn't know much about Chairman Mao or the way he governed China, but I remember village security men coming to my home every night to check our house for evidence of disloyalty to the party. I would be in the kitchen with my father when they came in, and I would go outside while they checked the house. This was just normal for me as a child. I was unaware of the seriousness of this act.

Before meals and before bed, we had to chant words of devotion and loyalty to Chairman Mao. I also remember the men of the village, including my brother, being called to a public room almost every night to practice being a soldier. Some of the women of the village periodically gathered to dance and sing for Chairman Mao.

My parents were very strict with us children—we were not allowed to speak, especially when there were visitors. I thought my parents were just being strict Chinese parents, but looking back, I recognize there was a background of fear.

My grandfather was co-opted as a doctor into the Communist Red Army. He loyally sacrificed for serving the country, but his family remained very poor while he served. When the war was over, my grandfather was falsely accused to being a "landlord," a very derogatory role under Communist rule. Sometimes people from the village would come to drag my grandfather out to shame him by beating him and making him wear a dunce hat. This accusation brought great pain and shame to the whole family. My mother learned how to be a doctor from her dad, but she could never go to school because of this shame.

My family background was Confucianism. My great-grandfather was a teacher who used a very thick textbook, San Zi Jing, to teach people how to live right. Our family was influenced by this Confucianism. So as a girl, I was taught that I should be quiet, do house chores, dance, and play the piano. As a general rule, men are taught to be honest and have a good heart; they should not be greedy and should do important things. Although we followed the practices of chanting Chairman Mao's sayings, my mother deeply influenced us from her understanding from San Zi Jing.

Although I grew up under these influences, I was very unaware of their impact. My stories give a glimpse of my family's cultural beliefs and practices and reveal God entering into my world. God began the process of changing my life values and reshaping my life.

HOW TO MAKE THE MOST OF THIS DEVOTIONAL

At the end of each day's reading I ask "What do you think?" Please feel free to write your own reflection and prayer in response to the day's reading.

一个美丽的"传说"

A Beautiful Legend or Something More?

He has made everything beautiful in its time. He has also set eternity in the hearts of men; yet they cannot fathom what God has done from beginning to end.

—Ecclesiastes 3:11

———————

My mother's father's father (my great- grandfather) was an elder-teacher in Hubei Province. He once told a legend to my mother, Lan Zhi Ying, while sitting in his shu fang (personal library).

He told her, "There is a beautiful place called Yidianyuan (paradise), and our ancestors used to live happily in this place. Then one day, they became a disobedient people and were cast out of Yidianyuan, into a world of suffering and misery—that is why we suffer today."

She asked, "Can we go back again?" He replied that when she turned about sixty years old, she would return. Was this prophetic? At age fifty-nine, she received Christ into her life. —

What Do You Think?

What early memories do you have of hearing about sin or about God?

Today's Reflection

_____
_____
_____
_____
_____
_____
_____
_____
_____
_____
_____
_____
_____
_____
_____
_____

Today's Prayer

_____
_____
_____
_____
_____

我的出生

Day 2

I Was Born

For you created my inmost being; you knit
me together in my mother's womb.
—Psalm 139:13

_____

My mother already had five sons and one daughter before I was born, and she agonized about having another child. She decided to abort me—not because I was a girl but because having another mouth to feed, in impoverished China, was more than she could bear.

My auntie talked my mom into keeping the child in her womb, saying, "You already have six. One more won't be too much! After this baby, then you should stop." This was reasonable to my mom, and she reversed her decision to abort me. Thank God for wise aunties around the world.

I'm amazed that while God knit me together in her womb, my dear mother struggled with psychological and social problems. Because she was desperate, abortion seemed to be the answer to her problems. God had other plans. –

4

What Do You Think?

What thoughts have you had about God's purpose for your birth?

Today's Reflection

_____

_____

_____

_____

_____

_____

_____

_____

_____

_____

_____

_____

_____

_____

_____

_____

Today's Prayer

_____

_____

_____

_____

_____

一条白手絹

A White Handkerchief

Man is like a breath; his days are
like a fleeting shadow.

—Psalm 144:4

When I was three years old, all the commotion and chaos in my house frightened me. It's all rather vague—I only remember impressions, except for all the wailing. Everyone was crying and wailing. My mother could not be comforted. I joined in the crying, not knowing what had happened or why I was crying. It was all vaguely sad to me.

When I was about ten years old, my mom sat me down and explained why my second brother was not returning home—it was then I learned what had happened seven years earlier. My brother and his girlfriend were found bound together with a white handkerchief, drowned in the river. The girlfriend's parents had forbidden them to see each other, and they chose to die rather than be apart.

In my memory, my brother is like a fleeting shadow. What he and his girlfriend did for love haunted me for such a long time. The power of romantic, forbidden love moved them to take their own lives—reckless youth! Grief visited my home, and the memory of that event cast a long shadow, until I wrestled with the love of Jesus Christ—a love that drove Him to sacrifice His life for me.

Unlike my brother's romantic love for his beautiful girlfriend, Jesus' love was a heroic sacrifice for an unlovely sinner. He died so that I might live an abundant life full of purpose and meaning in Him. He is all about life, not death. —

What Do You Think?

What events cast a long shadow over your life?

What events or people illustrated deep and abiding love?

Today's Reflection

_____
_____
_____
_____
_____
_____
_____
_____
_____
_____
_____
_____
_____
_____
_____

Today's Prayer

_____
_____
_____
_____
_____

"多生"的故事

Day 4

Sorry, Sarah, You Were Adopted

What is man that you are mindful of him,
the son of man that you care for him?
—Psalm 8:4

I was about five years old when I first heard from my brothers that I was adopted and not a real member of the Liu family. My third brother, Liu Xianzhong, first told me of my family status; then all four of my other brothers confirmed this shocking news. To them, it was a joke; to me, it was a disturbing revelation.

Chinese children are very sensitive about their family status. The difference between being natural-born and being adopted was an impossible chasm to bridge.

My father once bought clothes for the other children, but for some reason, nothing was bought for me. My brothers were wickedly quick to point out the reason why: "You are not one of us." Back then, it was enough to bring me to tears, but now I realize it was just a joke. I felt as though I was the extra child in the family— one that is least important. I felt like the disposable child.

In Christ, I have learned that as a Chinese girl (hence, a Gentile), I was adopted into God's family to share equally with the natural-born children (Jewish believers) and am granted the same worth and standing as those who are natural born. It took the blood of Christ to purchase me back to God—no small price! And I am eternally grateful. −

What Do You Think?

Words can leave a lasting impression. What words do you recall from your childhood that influenced your thoughts about yourself?

What specific words from God have influenced your sense of identity and value?

Today's Reflection

_____
_____
_____
_____
_____
_____
_____
_____
_____
_____
_____
_____
_____

Today's Prayer

_____
_____
_____
_____
_____
_____

我家的茅缸

Day 5

Forbidden Outhouse—
a Child's Curiosity

He raises the poor from the dust and
lifts the needy from the ash heap.
—Psalm 113:7

_____

"Stop! This is for adults, not kids!" they shouted at
me. But I was very curious. What was this thing that
I was forbidden from seeing?

In our humble village in China, we did not have
indoor restrooms. We had outhouses, but children
were not permitted in these outhouses. They had
other facilities that did not offer the privacy adults
required. The walls of the adult outhouse were made
from tightly bound branches and had an opening that
faced away from the house and toward unoccupied
land. There was no fear of exposure.

One summer afternoon after lunch, the entire family
lay down for a midday rest. While all were fast
asleep, I sneaked out of bed and out of my house
to the forbidden outhouse. I marveled over what I

saw—a little hideaway where the adults could relieve themselves. I found a commode that was a giant bowl with no running water. It was filled with human waste, but that didn't deter me. I climbed on the rim of the commode, to sit where adults sat, and I tried to take hold of two nearby posts to steady myself. All of a sudden, I lost my balance and fell into the commode—I was neck-deep in human waste! My sister discovered me and screamed, and the entire family came to my rescue. After that, I was not allowed to nap alone. I was made to nap between my two older brothers.

As a young adult, I fell into a greater mess than that old commode. The filth in my life was well over my head, and I was unable to pull myself from the sin and shame I brought to myself. It is true that God raised me and lifted me from the dust, ash, and dung of life. –

What Do You Think?

How has God raised you from the dust or removed you from the ash heap?

Today's Reflection

_____

_____

_____

_____

_____

_____

_____

_____

_____

_____

_____

_____

_____

_____

_____

_____

Today's Prayer

_____

_____

_____

_____

_____

別人說我"命大"

Ming Da! (Beyond Luck!) An Extraordinary Child

The Lord will keep you from all harm—
he will watch over your life.
—Psalm 121:7

It was almost wintertime. The sky was gray, and the wind howled through the house. But of course, this was not unusual. I was alone, as was often the case when the entire family was busy out in the fields. I typically was permitted to sleep later than everyone else did, as I was the youngest and could not help in the fields. My mother cooked breakfast on our wood- burning stove and stored my little breakfast in a pot that sat on the stove embers. I sleepily went to the stove and helped myself to my mom's deliciously hot, ready-to-eat meal. There I sat, next to the warm stove.

I was unaware that the wind had become extremely violent, and that our aging house was giving way. The roof, walls, and all suddenly crashed down around me. My neighbor half a block away saw the disaster and raced over to see if she could help. She came upon me, unhurt but trapped in the rubble. She sent word to my father, and he frantically came to my rescue. Later, I was told a rafter beam fell directly over my head but came short of striking me down because the beam lodged itself over me, with one end on the ground and the other end on the stove, creating a little shelter where I sat. Everyone exclaimed what an extremely lucky little child I was.

As a new Christian, I was told early on that there are no coincidences or luck in our lives. God takes care of us. Little did I know as an adult that I would be tested with calamity falling in all around me. Yet He keeps my life and His watchful eye on me in the shelter of His love. –

What Do You Think?

Looking back over your life, what events serve as evidence of God's protective care for you?

Today's Reflection

_____
_____
_____
_____
_____
_____
_____
_____
_____
_____
_____
_____
_____
_____
_____
_____
_____

Today's Prayer

_____
_____
_____
_____
_____

我的一片蓝天

My Blue Sky

Listen, my son [daughter], to your
father's instruction and do not
forsake your mother's teaching.
—Proverbs 1:8

I come from a strict Chinese family background—rules were very important. As a child, when I forgot the rules or disregarded the rules, I paid the consequence.

In my small village, I had several friends my age. While my family was away, working in the fields, I would host all my friends at my house, which my parents strictly forbade.

At about the age of six, after a hard day of play, my friends and I developed a fierce appetite. I ignored my mother's admonition, "Do not feed the entire village!"

I invited my friends to our vegetable garden to pick what they liked. Then we washed and sliced the vegetables and arranged them beautifully on our good family dish ware. After topping them off with a little oil and salt, we all ate our fill. To make things worse, we ate the rice that was prepared for the evening meal for the family. Once refreshed, we dashed out for more play.

When my family returned from a long day in the fields, my mom, angry at my disobedience, told me that if I liked my friends so much, I could go live with them. Then she began to push me to the door! In fear, I sobbed and begged not to be put out. I could not live without my mommy and daddy—I was sorry! They had always been my blue sky. How could I live without my blue sky?

My mommy never intended to put me out, just to frighten me into obedience. I know the Lord will never put me out, but when I sin, I emotionally revert to my childhood. I would do anything to stay close to my blue sky. Today, Jesus is my blue sky! I cannot live without him—lessons learned from my parents. –

What Do You Think?

What words do you use to describe your relationship with God, which keeps you walking carefully in obedience?

Today's Reflection

_____
_____
_____
_____
_____
_____
_____
_____
_____
_____
_____
_____
_____
_____
_____
_____
_____

Today's Prayer

_____
_____
_____
_____
_____

陪葬品

My Treasured Pencil Box

For he knows how we are formed, he
remembers that we are dust.
—Psalm 103:14

One of my earliest memories of kindergarten is of
the pencil box my daddy gave me. It was beautiful,
and I treasured it with all my heart. I took very good
care of it at school and home.

One day while at play, I heard wailing in my house. My
friends and I snuck over to the window as the wailing
grew louder and louder. What I saw shocked me,
although I didn't understand all that was happening.
My mom and oldest brother had returned from the
medical clinic, and I saw them holding my three-day-
old baby niece, uncontrollably crying and pacing
the floor. I rushed into the house, and although they
saw me, it was as if I was not present. They were
consumed by grief at the sudden death of the baby.

I joined in the chorus of wailing, all the way back
to my brother's home, where his young wife, who
suffered arthritis, was waiting for good news from
the doctors.

In rural China, funeral rites and burial happened the same day as the death. My brother obtained a small child-sized box to place my baby niece in, and the four of us buried her little body in the backyard. Before the little makeshift casket was let down, we all put gifts inside. And since I carried my treasured pencil box everywhere, I placed my greatest gift in her casket.

Again, as a child I was struck by our mortality. First, my second brother and now my baby niece. Life, I learned early on, is a fragile thing, like dust. From dust we were taken, and to it, we shall return. But thanks be to God that He gave us His Son, a gift far greater than any treasured pencil box, that we might live ... forever and ever! Amen! —

What Do You Think?

We are but dust. What events or things serve to remind you of the shortness of life?

Today's Reflection

_____
_____
_____
_____
_____
_____
_____
_____
_____
_____
_____
_____
_____
_____
_____
_____

Today's Prayer

_____
_____
_____
_____
_____

母亲的哭声吓着了我

Day 9

My Mom, Refusing to be Comforted

My heart is blighted and withered like grass;
I forget to eat my food. Because of my loud
groaning I am reduced to skin and bones.
—Psalm 102:4, 5

———————

Even as I write this, I am becoming more aware of my own sensitivity to life and death. I am prone to gravitate to a melancholy spirit.

Like most Chinese children, I am very attached to my mom, so whatever affects her, affects me.

Though loved by both of my parents (Dad, the spoiler, and Mom, the disciplinarian), I was closer to Mom. When her heart was shattered, so was mine, even though I didn't fully understand.

———————

Some Background

The Communist takeover of China in 1949 was a defining moment for my family. As previously mentioned, my grandfather was falsely accused of being a landlord, a status vehemently reproached by the Communist government. "Guilt by accusation" was the social norm, and no due process was available.

The government officials came down on our family, denying them any legal standing. Local officials shared in the government's condemnation of my family and relished the opportunity to humiliate them on every occasion.

The villagers were forced to make a public display of my grandfather by placing a dunce hat on his head and parading him up and down the village streets. Added to this humiliation was that my grandmother, as well as my mom and her siblings, were forced to stand with the jeering crowd. To my grandmother, this was reaching the limits of her ability to endure.

It was difficult enough to witness the unjust humiliation of the man she loved, but the injustice overflowed to her children. For my grandmother, life was utterly hopeless and unendurable. In the end, she drowned herself in a vat of water in her own humble kitchen. My mother would not be comforted in her grief. As a little child, I shared in that grief, to some extent. I discovered what it meant to be "blighted and withered like grass."

Only Jesus could lift me up from such hopelessness and despair and heal my family and me. I know now that the cycle of despair is broken. Thanks be to God, for He rescues us in Christ Jesus! —

What Do You Think?

How does a Christian's response to despair differ from a person's response to despair without Christ?

Today's Reflection

_____
_____
_____
_____
_____
_____
_____
_____
_____
_____
_____
_____
_____
_____
_____
_____
_____
_____
_____

Today's Prayer

_____
_____
_____
_____
_____
_____

Day 10

Given Away, Adopted by Another

As a father has compassion on his children, so
the Lord has compassion on those who fear him.

—Psalm 103:13

———————

I previously mentioned that my brothers told me
I was adopted. I now offer a bit more insight into
those days—a little excursion to my mind-set as a
child

As I looked at my family, three things suggested
to me, unwittingly, that I was simply "extra" and
unnecessary baggage. First, my family was very
poor, and a seventh child is an unnecessary financial
burden. Second, my family had enough boys (five
sons). Third, my older sister satisfied the female-
gender quota. This left me as extra baggage. I'm not
saying that my thoughts were right, but that was my
childish reasoning.

This gets a bit complicated. My grand- auntie, a central
figure in my life, who was better off financially than

our family, wanted me to stay with her adopted adult son. He already had two sons, but his wife wanted a daughter. My parents made the arrangements, and I was sent to their home.

To the best of my recollection, my stay with my new family was good, yet with every passing day of my absence, my father grew more miserable and regretted his decision to let me go.

After one month, my father could no longer live without me, and he marched eight miles to my cousin's house and pleaded with him and his wife to allow me to return home. They agreed, and all the way home, my father held me tightly and expressed regret over letting me go. That day, I knew I was his daughter.

The next time I felt this sort of unrelenting love was when I received Christ into my life. He carried me all the way to my heavenly Father. To this day, He tells me I am His, and He will not let me go! —

What Do You Think?

How has God expressed His unrelenting love to you?

Today's Reflection

_____

_____

_____

_____

_____

_____

_____

_____

_____

_____

_____

_____

_____

_____

_____

_____

_____

_____

Today's Prayer

_____

_____

_____

_____

_____

淹不死的我

Day 11

"Meimei Is Drowning!"

Do not let the floodwaters engulf me or the depths swallow me up or the pit close its mouth over me.
—Psalm 69:15

My two older brothers wanted to go to the lake for a late-afternoon swim and bath, but my sister, whom I called Jiejie (older sister) and I—known as Meimei, or younger sister, to my siblings—were left in their care while Dad and Mom were away. More than anything, I wanted to be with my brothers and their friends. I wanted to hang out with the big kids. I was tired of always being referred to as the annoying "little kid."

In full knowledge that my parents would disapprove, my brothers took us to the lake. How proud I felt, walking with the big kids.

As they went into the deep water, my brothers sternly warned us to stay on the lake's edge or, at most, to go in no farther than ankle-deep water. Well, I was a big kid now, so I ventured out deeper, and deeper, and deeper, until I couldn't touch the bottom, and I sank like a rock. My sister, in desperation, screamed for my brothers to help me.

I can recall going down into the deep water in an utter panic, sucking in water while gasping for air. I was in sheer terror, wildly flinging my arms and legs, and then ... nothing.

When I regained consciousness, my brothers, their friend, and Jiejie were all leaning over me. As I recall the hurried discussion by the lake, my brothers were genuinely concerned for me, which made me both happy and proud of them. And they pleaded with me, by way of candy bribes and threats of exclusion, not to tell Dad and Mom what had happened to me.

When the psalmist describes the drowning moment, my mind instantly goes back to this moment. When I heard the gospel, I became keenly aware that I was drowning in my lake of sin, where no big brothers could save me. With unceasing tears and desperation, I cried out to Jesus, and He rescued me. The despair of my heart was replaced by gratitude and joy. No bribes or threats thereafter; nothing more was required. –

What Do You Think?

Have you experienced times in your life when you felt you were overwhelmed and close to "drowning"? How did you escape? Who helped you?

Today's Reflection

_____

_____

_____

_____

_____

_____

_____

_____

_____

_____

_____

_____

_____

_____

_____

_____

Today's Prayer

_____

_____

_____

_____

_____

母亲对死去奶奶的孝心

Day 12

A Placebo

Arise, O Lord! Deliver me, O my God!"
—Psalm 3:7a

Chinese bereavement customs, at best, are grasping at air. After my grandmother's suicide, my mother was inconsolable. Ancient Chinese custom has it that the spirits of the dead remain in our midst. We can still serve them and make a display of offerings and provide for them.

My mom set out to construct a house and clothing from plum-colored paper for my deceased grandmother. She invited me to help her in the project. I could see the grief and sorrow in her face as she cut out all the several parts. My mom meticulously cut out several doll-size tops and pants for her mom, and then when the clothing was complete, she constructed a miniature house with the same paper. This project took most of the day.

When all was made ready, we traveled to the field and to a large tree that served as a landmark for where my grandmother was buried. As Chinese custom dictates, we set off a string of firecrackers to announce our arrival. I will never forget the look on my mother's face as she lovingly and painfully offered the clothes and house to my grandmother by lighting it on fire, and all the while, she wept and told Grandmother that she came to provide for her. At the conclusion of this bizarre ceremony, we lit another string of firecrackers to announce our departure.

When we were preparing these gifts for Grandmother, I questioned my mother about this ancient practice. "Will Grandmother really wear the clothes?" I asked. "Will she really live in this house?" No doubt, my mom could detect the incredulity in my voice. She said she really didn't know, but that it made her feel better.

As a child, my very own Chinese traditions put seeds of doubt in my heart, and those seeds grew and bloomed in my young adult life. Religion was a placebo, something made up to make us feel better —that is, until I encountered the living God, who is bigger than life itself. He is a real deliverer and comforter to those who put their trust in Him. —

What Do You Think?

When did you first become aware of serious questions about life and death?

Today's Reflection

_____

_____

_____

_____

_____

_____

_____

_____

_____

_____

_____

_____

_____

_____

_____

_____

_____

_____

Today's Prayer

_____

_____

_____

_____

_____

四哥为什么流泪

Shattered Dreams and Irony

Your righteousness is like the mighty
mountains, your justice like the great deep.
O Lord, you preserve both man and beast.
—Psalm 36:6

I had a special fondness for my fourth brother. When everyone else would overlook me, my brother would seek me out.

As long as I could remember, my brother was talented and thoughtful in the most marvelous way. As a young man, he was multitalented. He played traditional Chinese instruments and had an entrepreneurial spirit that turned our home into a breakfast club. He could keep anyone entertained, especially me. I also admired him for his good-natured thoughtfulness and easygoing manner.

In our house, after dinner and when homework was finished, we'd all sit down to play card games. Being the youngest also meant I was left out. After all, who wants an incompetent little kid on their team? My brother did. I knew if he was my game partner, he wouldn't yell at me if I made a mistake. Nothing I did would trouble him; he made light of my childish incompetence. Even in real life, he took all manner of difficulties in stride, with a healthy dose of humor. He took others seriously, but he didn't take himself seriously.

His dream was to go to university and become something more than a lowly villager. My dad and mom pinned their hopes on our generation, and my brother showed every promise to succeed.

One night, I sought out my brother when it was game-playing time, but he was nowhere to be found. I quietly opened his bedroom door, and my eyes immediately glanced at the head of his bed next to the desk, where I expected him to be. When my eyes adjusted to the darkness, I could clearly see that he had been crying, as the tears still lingered on his face. As in other emotional situations, my heart immediately broke—he was my close brother, and I had a special affinity to him. Later, I would discover what happened.

As previously described, my grandfather's being accused of being a landlord caused persecution by government and local officials. These wicked officials had a very long memory—so long, that when my brother interviewed with his high school teacher about his future for university, he was told that he had no future at university, even though my brother knew his grades far exceeded the state's requirement. This shattered his dreams and further crushed my parents' spirit.

The irony is that in today's evolving China, my brother is a land manager. That is to say that although the property ultimately belongs to the state, the state gives my brother all the privileges and rights, much like a landowner in a capitalist state. He is, for all practical purposes, a landlord and highly respected by both government and local officials for his skills.

From my perspective here in America, I rejoice over my evolving China, albeit in a limited way, and I celebrate that my brother's shattered dreams have been mended. Thanks be to a just God, who is able to preserve my beloved family. —

What Do You Think?

Have you mended shattered dreams? Are there disappointments that have played a crucial role in your life?

Today's Reflection

Today's Prayer

手无分文，随她的命吧

Day 14

"We Have No Money!"

A thousand may fall at your side, ten thousand at
your right hand, but it will not come near you.

—Psalm 91:7

When I was almost ten years old, I was stricken
with an acute jaundice condition. I recall that the
wheat harvest was already completed, and it was
a weekend during rice harvest time. My father and
brothers were returning from a long, hard day in
the fields, and I was with my mom at home. I recall
having severe abdominal pains, and I went to my
mom, a trained medical professional. She took one
look at me and knew my condition was serious.

My eyes and skin were jaundiced yellow, and I could
see the alarm in my mom's face. In today's medicine,
jaundice can be treated easily enough, but in my
childhood days, jaundice, if untreated or under
treated, could be fatal.

My father was faced with a dilemma, because, as he
exclaimed, "We have no money!" In despair, as the
primary provider for the family, he surrendered me

to fate. "If she lives, she lives; if she dies, she dies." But my mom and brothers argued with my dad—they were not about to commit me to fate. They insisted that I be taken to the hospital, which was some distance down the road. We had only a village clinic, which was unprepared for my condition. My brother raced back to the fields and converted a one-axle trailer to a bicycle-pulled ambulance, in which they transported me—with enormous effort and urgency—to the hospital.

Upon arrival, my mom's diagnosis was confirmed; I had an acute case of jaundice.

The receiving doctor told my mom and brothers that they arrived just in time. My condition was so severe that I was borderline for non admittance, meaning that even the medical professionals would have given up on me and sent me home to die. But as it was, they saw a glimmer of hope and hospitalized me in isolation for a month. When I returned home, I was directed to stay in bed. I could not resume my school activities, and therefore, I was set back a year due to my illness and absence.

Psalm 91 reminded me that I was one of those who did not fall by way of pestilence and plague. By the grace of God, a fast- acting family, and a hopeful doctor, my life stands as a testament to His goodness. How merciful is our God and Lord Jesus Christ! –

What Do You Think?

What memories or thoughts are triggered when you read these words from Psalm 91: "A thousand may fall at your side, ten thousand at your right hand, but it will not come near you"?

Today's Reflection

_____
_____
_____
_____
_____
_____
_____
_____
_____
_____
_____
_____
_____
_____
_____
_____

Today's Prayer

_____
_____
_____
_____
_____
_____

家庭的瓶颈

Day 15

Impoverished and Possessed

They worshiped their idols, which
became a snare to them.
—Psalm 106:36

Xianxiu, my older sister by three years (whom I
called Jiejie) was a beautiful and fashionable young
lady. Though a village girl, she was a trendsetter
for our small community. But one day, she instantly
changed frightfully—for the worse.

My mom knew that whatever possessed my sister
was not a physical condition but a spiritual one. My
entire family is not, by nature, superstitious, so this
event took us all by surprise and left us desperately
searching for answers.

Some of the village women told my mom that my
sister was possessed by a demon and that she
needed to call on the local spiritualist to exorcise
the demon. So my mom traveled to another village
in search of the spiritualist. The spiritualist was an
old lady who demanded several conditions be met
in order to exorcise the demon. First, a room in our

home, where a small shrine was built and incensed burned, was to be set apart for the demon to be welcomed. Next, we were to set aside the first and the fifteenth of the month to invite the spiritualist and her cohorts to take over our home to conduct spiritual rituals to appease the demon. We were to buy them all new outfits to wear for these special occasions and supply the best meals for them all. Finally, we were made to pay large sums of money to them, which broke the back of my family's finances and reduced our home to bare survival.

I recall when my brother once sent me to spy on the spiritualists as they performed their incantations. Through the crack in the door, I could see my sister passed out on the floor and the spiritualists standing over her, making gestures with their arms for the demon to go away. They would shout my sister's name and say, "Come back! Come back!" What I saw and heard gave me the creeps, and I raced back to my brothers to report all that I witnessed.

My sister's condition never improved, and our family went deeper into poverty. There seemed to be no way out. —

What Do You Think?

How do you explain sickness that is not physical? Where do people generally turn for help?

Today's Reflection

_____
_____
_____
_____
_____
_____
_____
_____
_____
_____
_____
_____
_____
_____
_____
_____
_____
_____

Today's Prayer

_____
_____
_____
_____
_____

姐姐邀我去烧香

Day 16

Invited into Darkness

They know nothing, they understand nothing.
They walk about in darkness; all the
foundations of the earth are shaken.
—Psalm 82:5

A strange development occurred while my sister was in this condition. She was made a spiritualist herself. She became a keeper of the dark room in our home. She would maintain the shrine and burn incense regularly. Village people even came to seek her counsel and incantations to help them in their troubles. Our home became headquarters for the Devil.

I remember one day, when my parents were away, my sister bade me to come into the dark room with her. She thoroughly frightened me and just going into that room was even more frightening—it was all my childhood fears rolled up into one. I was to walk into the Devil's den.

But somehow, I reasoned that perhaps my cooperation with my sister would lead to her healing. So I mustered all my courage and followed her into the dark room. There, she instructed me to burn incense and a special paper dedicated for the purpose of incantations. We bowed down before the shrine, and my sister mumbled words I could not comprehend.

Eventually, my sister completed her rituals and got up off her knees. That was all the signal I needed to jump up and dart out of the room before her. That was totally creepy! I thought. I never want to put myself in that situation again. I was spiritually ignorant and walking in darkness. The foundation of my life had been shaken. —

What Do You Think?

What experiences have you had that shook the foundations of what you believe?

Today's Reflection

_____
_____
_____
_____
_____
_____
_____
_____
_____
_____
_____
_____
_____
_____
_____
_____
_____
_____

Today's Prayer

_____
_____
_____
_____
_____
_____

耶穌介入了我家

Day 17

When Jesus Visited My Home

Hope deferred makes the heart sick, but
a longing fulfilled is a tree of life.
—Proverbs 13:12

Some of my mother's relatives came to us after about a year into the futile exercise with my sister. They'd heard about my older sister's condition and brought the gospel to my mom. My mom thought at first that she would have to do more elaborate things for this Jesus, which would make our situation even more intolerable. But her relatives encouraged her to believe in the Lord Jesus Christ and that He would heal my sister.

This was the same family that had taken me in many years earlier (the cousin and his wife who wanted a daughter). After I returned home, one of the cousin's sons later became demon-possessed, doing terrible violence and demonstrating great strength. But he was miraculously healed by the Lord. Soon, they all became Christians and even built a house church building in dedication to the Lord Jesus.

This Jesus, who cast out devils, now came to our home and brought healing to my dear Jiejie.

The healing was not instant, however, but gradual. Today, my sister is completely healed and in her right mind. How sinister and evil is the enemy of our souls to ensnare the unsuspecting and the unlearned by promising what it will not deliver, and deliver what we do not want! Our God is able to deliver us from even demonic snares. With my mom becoming the first Christian in our family and village, Jesus now took up permanent residence. My mom became an unshakeable stronghold of faith because of what Jesus had said and done in healing my sister.

Calling on the spiritualist deferred our hope and vanquished our family finances. Jesus healed my sister and made my mom alive like a Tree of Life. —

What Do You Think?

How has God used difficult situations in your family to bring fresh hope like a Tree of Life?

Today's Reflection

_____
_____
_____
_____
_____
_____
_____
_____
_____
_____
_____
_____
_____
_____
_____
_____
_____
_____

Today's Prayer

_____
_____
_____
_____
_____

我要退学

A Bitter Lot Came Home to Stay

May the day of my birth perish, and the night it was said, "A boy [girl] is born!"
—Job 3:3

The role of education in Chinese culture is vastly important—it is the only way out of a life of misery. The hopes of parents are pinned on the next generation's ability to do and be better. I shared in this dream, until ...

Fate has dealt me a bitter blow! I thought as I peddled eight miles home from school on my bicycle. Jiejie's episode with the Devil had delivered a devastating blow to our family finances. I finally came to the harsh realization that there was no money left for me to live on campus and complete my education. The dream stopped with me.

It was two weeks before the end of term, and while all my classmates were in class, I sneaked back to my dorm to pack up in secret. My emotions at that moment were complicated, as there wasn't any reason for the secrecy.

I gathered all my possessions in a blanket and placed the bundle on my back. I got on my bike and peddled away from the school, away from my friends, and away from my future and dreams.

When I read the words from Job, I recalled the sadness I experienced as I rode the last dusty stretch of road. Like Job, I also questioned why I was born, and I cursed my life. —

What Do You Think?

Have you ever experienced the kind of deep sadness that caused you to question why you were born? What was your response?

Today's Reflection

_____

_____

_____

_____

_____

_____

_____

_____

_____

_____

_____

_____

_____

_____

_____

_____

Today's Prayer

_____

_____

_____

_____

_____

重返学校

Day 19

Compelled to Complete Middle School

He has made everything beautiful in its time. He has also set eternity in the hearts of men; yet they cannot fathom what God has done from beginning to end.
—Ecclesiastes 3:11

When I arrived back home, I was met by my sister, who could read the expression on my face. I told her I was home for good and would not return to school. She pleaded with me to return but to no avail. She cried out and said if she could, she would pay my way back. But we both knew no resources were available for either of us. The unspoken reality between the two of us was that Dad and Mom spent all they had trying to help her. Now, nothing was left for me. No one felt worse than my sister did.

That night, my parents came home from the fields, and my sister whispered to them that I had returned from school and had no intention of completing the term. My parents rushed in and pleaded with me to return to school. I argued with them and said, "We have no money!" How could I possibly return? Again, they pleaded with me, saying that they'd find the money some way, somehow. I stubbornly turned a deaf ear to them, no longer listening to their pleas. I was brokenhearted and so were they. Great sadness overcame my family.

The next day, I was taken by surprise. Late in the morning, there was a commotion in my house. My sister ran into my room to tell me that my school friends had come to see me. In disbelief, I went into the living room to find at least ten of my close friends and classmates standing there, waiting to speak with me. The moment I saw them, I knew why they had come—to convince me to return to school.

My sister, doing all in her power to help matters, hurried to prepare lunch for all our guests. They immediately launched into telling me all the reasons for me to return. "Everyone is missing you. The teachers are asking for you. You only have two weeks left! Who knows what will happen after school ends? Perhaps money will come to you." And with many other words, they eventually persuaded me to return, yet in my heart of hearts, I thought, Why? Who knows the beginning from the end? —

What Do You Think?

What memories or thoughts come to your mind when you read these words, "He has made everything beautiful in its time"?

Today's Reflection

_____
_____
_____
_____
_____
_____
_____
_____
_____
_____
_____
_____
_____
_____
_____

Today's Prayer

_____
_____
_____
_____
_____

高中开学的第一天

Day 20

The First Day of High School

Whatever wisdom may be, it is far off and
most profound— who can discover it?
—Ecclesiastes 7:24

"It's almost nine! He should be here by now!" There I sat in front of my house, waiting for my brother, who had promised to take me to register for high school. After I completed my middle-school exams, I was honored to receive an invitation to attend high school. This honor was not automatic in China. One was required to qualify.

I was wearing my first-day-of-school best and anticipating meeting up with all my friends and meeting new friends. I could imagine the encounters and the happiness of the moment. Where is he? I thought. I'm going to be late!

My brother drove up on his motorcycle, and I was prepared to jump in the passenger seat and take off. But he got off his motorcycle and said he wanted to speak with me. I sensed something wrong and braced myself. He told me that he must attend a meeting and would not be able to take me to registration day at the high school. I was in utter disbelief. We had talked about this day, and he knew what it meant to me!

He then told me that I should forget about school, because he could find me a good- paying job locally. I was in shock! I couldn't believe what I was hearing. There he stood, trying to advise me away from my education for the instant gratification of work and a paycheck. Did he know what he was talking about? Does anybody know what they're talking about? I knew it was because we had no money for my education. That which I feared had come upon me. On that day, I decided I would take matters into my own hands. I would listen to no one's counsel but my own.

Numbed by this event, I turned away from my brother and silently went into my room, wearing my first-day-of-school best and carrying my broken dreams. What was I to do now? Why was wisdom so far off? —

What Do You Think?

Can you recall a situation in which your dreams were broken and wisdom seemed so far away? What was your response?

Today's Reflection

_____
_____
_____
_____
_____
_____
_____
_____
_____
_____
_____
_____
_____
_____
_____
_____

Today's Prayer

_____
_____
_____
_____
_____

破灭的梦

Day 21

Life without a Dream

My life is consumed by anguish and my years
by groaning; my strength fails because of
my affliction, and my bones grow weak.

—Psalm 31:10

"Where is she?" My family probably said this to one another when they realized I wasn't at home. I had run away to my auntie's house. I gave no notice and received no permission. I felt it was the only thing I could do when confronted with my new reality— shattered dreams.

My family did everything in their power, short of providing for my education, to make life better for me. All of them, individually and collectively, tried to cheer me up and give me hope. But I simply would not be comforted. Eventually, all their words became a bitter reminder of my broken hopes and dreams. I was spiraling downward into deep depression. The only thing I could do to save my sanity was to run away from my circumstances and enter into another environment. I knew my auntie would take me in, and she did just that. She told my mother immediately that I was with her, and my mom and family gave me the time and space to work through my disappointment.

My auntie operated a simple family breakfast place, and I started helping her with the business. She taught me how to start up the eatery every morning at 5:30. The local customers would arrive at 6:00 a.m., and sometimes the eatery would stay open late at night.

For three months, I lived with my auntie and worked with her at the eatery. It didn't improve my emotional state, but it didn't make it worse. It kept me distracted. My mom appealed to my auntie, who was my mom's best friend and a close friend of the family, to send me home. But I stubbornly refused. Later, my sister came to me and appealed to me to return. I relented and went back home. Once again, depression overtook me.

After returning home, I refused to do anything constructive. I must have been impossible to live with, as I spent most of my day watching soap operas and reading novels. I also started to keep a diary with random notes, picture cutouts from magazines, and poems handwritten from books.

I would occasionally walk down to the field and sit among the tall grass, anguishing over my situation. What was I to do? My short, brief life had come to an end. I recall taking strolls to the river and just crying my eyes out, tears flowing in utter despair because I had no future. Suicidal thoughts tempted me to jump in the river and end it all.

I look back now and think how different life would have been at that moment if I had known the Lord Jesus. He could have saved me from the deep depression and emotional weakness I struggled with back then. My God is health and wholeness for the brokenhearted! –

What Do You Think?

What people have encouraged you when you were very discouraged?

What things do you do to cope with deep discouragement?

Today's Reflection

_____
_____
_____
_____
_____
_____
_____
_____
_____
_____
_____
_____
_____
_____

Today's Prayer

_____
_____
_____
_____
_____

真的有鬼

The Devil Is Real

By the word of the Lord were the heavens made,
their starry host by the breath of his mouth.
—Psalm 33:6

_____

As a young unbeliever, I never thought much about God or devils until these sinister events visited my home. Now, I found myself confronted by spiritual entities and forces, before which I was powerless. If I encountered a prowler, I could try to defend myself. If someone wronged me, I could try to seek justice. But what recourse is there before spiritual realities beyond our comprehension?

My mom and sister both believed in Jesus—and both were the laughing stock of the village. My mom, whom I love dearly, could not carry a tune. Yet she and my sister loved singing the songs of the church at the top of their lungs!

Every Sunday morning at daybreak, my mom and sister would be off to a church meeting, miles away, carrying their backpacks filled with notebooks, pens, and food for the day. They would return at dusk from their meeting. It was bad enough that the entire village could see them coming and going to church on a day when most people were home enjoying the weekend, but they added to our family humiliation by singing loudly as they walked. Everyone—including me—mocked them for their silly efforts, saying, "Look! The college girls with their backpacks have returned!" They made me so ashamed.

One day, when my family was away, my sister had episodes of spiritual battles that absolutely frightened me. Although Jesus had done a marvelous healing on my sister—a fact my unbelieving heart resisted— she would still have an occasional episode of tumultuous conflict within, as the Devil tried to reclaim the soul that Jesus had freed. During one of those episodes, she cried out for me to help her. I was at a complete loss as to what to do. She instructed me to read the words of a song that summarized the life of our Lord, from incarnation to ascension. Even though I was in an unbelieving state, I did as she said, simply because I wanted to do all in my power to help her.

What I saw next amazed me. One minute, she was in anguish and turmoil; soon after my reading to her, she was at peace and in her right mind. So startling was the contrast that in my heart of hearts, something started to happen in me, even though I did all in my power to suppress it.

Playing a small role and watching the power of God at work left a lasting impression. His Word is powerful beyond comprehension. –

What Do You Think?

When did you first experience the power of God's Word?

Today's Reflection

_____
_____
_____
_____
_____
_____
_____
_____
_____
_____
_____
_____
_____
_____
_____
_____
_____
_____

Today's Prayer

_____
_____
_____
_____
_____

人生的句号

Day 23

Gray Hair—Black Hair

He shot his arrows and scattered the enemies,
great bolts of lightning and routed them.

—Psalm 18:14

As life settled into routine, I found myself dwelling on my broken dreams and empty life. I reflected on the fact that all I truly loved in the world was my parents. There was no one else I loved more than them— no best friend or boyfriends. Chinese custom forbade any open romance between boys and girls my age, but I had no interest in boys at that time. They didn't occupy my thoughts at all. My parents, however, were another story. They were the world to me.

In one of those episodes of deep despair and depression, I sat down and wrote:

> I don't want to live.
> I live in continual, unbearable sorrow.
> I realize I live this way by choice. You
> have lost one son already, and
> now you will lose me.

"Gray hair [my aging parents] bury the black hair [their adult child]" was the idiom I used to describe what ought not to be. It is the young who bury the elderly, not the other way around. Yet once again, they were about to experience gray-hair-to- black-hair grief.

> You will be sad for a season
> I see no way out

To my sister and brothers, I beg you to take up my part in support of our parents

"There—I finished the letter," I said to myself as I signed and dated it. My letter was intended to clearly indicate suicide. My death must not be mistaken for homicide or abduction. I didn't want my parents to have any false hopes about my whereabouts or cause of death. This letter would put an end to any speculation.

The typical hiding place, where space was respected, was under my pillow. There would be those moments when curiosity would get the best of me, and I would sneak to see what was under my sister's pillow. This time, my sister's curiosity got the best of her—or was she shot like an arrow from the hand of God to scatter the enemies of my soul? She found the letter and immediately, without my knowledge, showed my parents.

Although we never spoke about the letter, there was no doubt in my mind that everyone in the household knew what I had written. From that point on, I was never left alone. My primary watcher was my dear Jiejie. The entire family watched my every move to protect me from myself.

This episode eventually passed, but my emotional state did not dramatically improve—at least not yet. –

What Do You Think?

In what ways do you express your sorrow and discouragement? How aware are others of your negative feelings?

Today's Reflection

_____

_____

_____

_____

_____

_____

_____

_____

_____

_____

_____

_____

_____

_____

_____

_____

_____

Today's Prayer

_____

_____

_____

_____

_____

母亲的祷告

My Mother's Prayer

I call on you, O God, for you will answer
me; give ear to me and hear my prayer.
—Psalm 17:6

I heard sobbing in the predawn hours, and I did not know what was happening. This became a regular event in our home. I knew it was my mother who was sobbing, and I thought, how burdened she must be with all the misfortunes of her life.

One day I heard my mom sobbing and talking to someone in her room. I quietly opened the door and slipped in to find out what was going on, when all of a sudden, in the midst of her groaning, she said my name, even though she was not addressing me. Who is she speaking to? I thought. I slipped out after I realized she was praying to Jesus for me.

I became the focus of her prayer life. The suicide letter they discovered and the fact that my sister was dramatically healed allowed her to turn her prayer life toward me. Today, I understand this in the wonderful light of the Lord, but back then, I cynically thought,

Who is she talking to? Isn't she just babbling in the air? Yes, I was in desperate need of my mother's prayers, even though I was ignorant and blind to the spiritual realities she clearly perceived.

Just as she labored physically to bring me into the world, now she was laboring again, in prayer, to bring me into the kingdom of heaven.

Jesus heard my mother's prayer. Little did I know, life was about to change in ways my small imagination could not fathom. –

What Do You Think?

What are your first memories and impressions of prayer? What people have played a role in demonstrating prayer to you?

Today's Reflection

_____
_____
_____
_____
_____
_____
_____
_____
_____
_____
_____
_____
_____
_____
_____
_____
_____
_____

Today's Prayer

_____
_____
_____
_____
_____

耶稣正在靠近我

Jesus Closing In on Me

The Lord is close to the brokenhearted and
saves those who are crushed in spirit.
—Psalm 34:18

———————

My mom had now turned her whole attention on winning me to Christ. But I was a hard nut to crack! Nevertheless, my mom was as "shrewd as a serpent." My sister's life had grown more and more productive, and she was moving on with life, while I was still floundering in unbelief and without purpose.

Mom saw that I was totally bored with life and asked if I would attend church with her and my sister. I shot that down immediately. I'm bored but not that bored!

I thought. Then she subtly shifted her strategy, saying, "We have an ancient book at church, and no one can read it. With the reading skills you have, why don't you join us as a reader?"

Nice try, Mom, but that wasn't going to work. I simply was not going to become another neighborhood joke, like she and my sister had become. Church was out of the question.

She finally wore me down by saying, "Now that your sister is busy with her life, please copy down the lyrics of our church songs for me here at home." This was much more reasonable. I could be a respectful daughter and not appear a fool to the village. So I agreed. After all, what harm could there be in it?

There I sat with paper and pen, copying one song after another for my mother. But as I copied these lyrics, I found myself absorbed in the language and imagery the songs had expressed. Beautiful, I thought, simply beautiful. But could this be true?

Something was happening inside me. These words talked about joy and peace in the presence of the Lord. They talked about Jesus always being with us. They promised a beautiful life here and in heaven after life. Could this be true or only the lively imagination of the gullible? I wanted it to be true, but from where I was standing—in spiritual darkness—it just seemed incomprehensible.

Jesus was closing in on me. Hallelujah! –

What Do You Think?

What do you recall about God's early working in your heart to draw you to Him? What people played a role in God's process?

Today's Reflection

_____

_____

_____

_____

_____

_____

_____

_____

_____

_____

_____

_____

_____

_____

_____

_____

_____

_____

Today's Prayer

_____

_____

_____

_____

_____

被孤独所困

Day 26

When the Singing Stopped

From birth I was cast upon you; from my
mother's womb you have been my God.
—Psalm 22:10

Jiejie and I went through what all close sisters
went through: sharing secrets, fighting, making up,
accusing and falsely accusing, making up again, and
being stubborn and being proud, yet unable to live
apart from each other because we would ... make
up, again.

Now added to all this was the demonic crisis she
went through in which Jesus delivered her from the
lion's teeth. A familiar sound around our home was
my sister's singing. After Jesus restored her, my sister
would sing songs of the church all day long. I recall
tolerating her singing and most of the time ignoring
the message the songs contained. But there were
those moments, unbeknownst to my sister, when
I would find myself reflecting on the message she
sang. Then, as quickly as I would reflect, I would
dismiss it.

My sister's life was dramatically improving. She was constantly joyful and full of hope. And then a young man came into her life. Nature ran its course, and the wedding day came.

Chinese wedding customs are unlike American wedding customs. Friends and relatives of the bride are invited to the bride's home for a two-day celebration in anticipation of the wedding. At sunset on day two of the celebration, the groom comes to the bride's home. He is bearing gifts and has an entourage of his friends and family, which is announced by fireworks as they come down the village path. He has also hired a band (drums, cymbals, and horns) of joy makers. One additional and very important person also is with the groom—a "wise" man. This wise man is skilled in the art of navigating through the possibility of old family disputes and/or disapprovals.

The bride's family comes out to receive the groom's entourage with cheers and applause and corresponding fireworks. Upon arrival, the bride's joy-making band answers the groom's joy-making band. This exchange happens for a couple of hours.

Then a meal is prepared for all guests and family. Tables are set up inside and outside the bride's home, with decorations marking the celebration. After this meal, the bride is sent off with her groom to conclude the wedding ritual at his home— by bicycle. Dressed in her special red good-luck dress, the bride side straddles the bike frame as the groom walks the bike with his new bride through the village of well-wishers. The bride and groom make their way through the village crowds by creating amusing, festive distractions, such as tossing candy away from the road or setting off firecrackers to create an opening in the midst of the crowd.

The full weight of my sister's absence was beginning to crash in on me. At the end of the meal at our home, she made her grand exit from our bedroom to be received by her husband at our front door. Between the bedroom exit and her reaching the front door, I spontaneously rushed to her and threw my arms around her, refusing to let her go. We both sobbed, and no words were exchanged. I would not hear her beautiful voice singing the songs of the church anymore. Jiejie was starting her new life, and I was going to be alone. I raced toward their bicycle and took hold of it, determined not to let her go. I cried out loud, not for joy but for the coming grief of her absence. Eventually, I was pulled away, and they were permitted to leave.

No sister and no songs ringing in the air of our home. I was truly alone—or so I thought, in my still-unbelieving mind. I look back now and see my Lord standing there the whole time. From the womb, to birth, through life, up until now. Praise be to God— never alone! –

What Do You Think?

Which wedding traditions express the joy of celebration in your culture, and which help to bring closure? How do such family events affect you?

Today's Reflection

_____

_____

_____

_____

_____

_____

_____

_____

_____

_____

_____

_____

_____

_____

_____

_____

Today's Prayer

_____

_____

_____

_____

_____

Day 27

I Challenged My Mom's Lord

O Lord God Almighty, who is like you?
You are mighty, O Lord, and your
faithfulness surrounds you.
—Psalm 89:8

My mom and I drew closer together after my sister went off to her married life. She found more occasions to talk to me about Jesus, which always made me feel uncomfortable.

One day she was boasting about how almighty God was and that He could do anything. "Well, if God can do anything," I retorted, holding out my hands, "let Him pour money into my hands!" How patient my mother was with a foolish daughter such as me. She went away to pray for me, as I demanded that her almighty God do something.

Upon her return, I simply would not let it go. "If God can do anything, I want to be tall!"—another totally unreasonable request to be spent on my own vanity and pleasure. Money and beauty! What more could anyone want? Yet her almighty God, who could do anything, couldn't do my simple request. My mom endured my folly, which only made her pray more fervently.

I have to admit that to this day, I am still without money and barely five feet tall, but I am one very contented woman in His almighty care. —

What Do You Think?

What doubts did you have before coming to Christ?
Did you ever challenge God?

Today's Reflection

_____

_____

_____

_____

_____

_____

_____

_____

_____

_____

_____

_____

_____

_____

_____

_____

_____

Today's Prayer

_____

_____

_____

_____

_____

被邀参加 Party!

Day 28

Invited to a Party!

[Wisdom calls,] "Let all who are
simple come in here!"
—Proverbs 9:4

————————

My near relatives came by the house and invited me to a party. I knew these relatives were Christian and that they were truly devoted to the Lord. I innocently accepted and got ready to go to their home with them, where the party was going to take place. My mom encouraged me to join them. As I look back now, I believe that my mom and my relatives plotted this event all along. I was blind to it.

They requested that I bring extra clothing, which I thought a little unusual, but they were my relatives, and my mom gave her consent, so I gathered up some extra clothing, and my relatives and I walked eight miles to their home. We arrived in the early evening and waited for nightfall. Then we set off for the party.

As we approached the house where the party was to take place, I looked through the entrance and was

86

confused about what I saw—a large room, practically empty of any furnishing, with dry rice stalks evenly distributed over the floor and overlaid with sheets for people to sit on. Men and women sat in separate seating arrangements. And to my amazement, there sat my mom. That was when I realized they had plotted together to get me there. I was not angry or upset; I was deeply curious.

As we entered, they were singing songs of worship, led by an evangelist in the front. I became aware that something was at work in me—something beyond description, something that made me forget about myself. The novelty of the moment captivated me, and I took a seat and listened intently to all they said.

This was a gospel meeting for unbelievers, and I was part of it—and remained part of it for the next three days! Wisdom used my near relatives and my mom to bring me to a place where I could receive from the Lord. I braced myself for what would come next. —

What Do You Think?

What efforts were made by others to bring you to Christ?

What efforts have you made to bring others to Christ?

Today's Reflection

_____
_____
_____
_____
_____
_____
_____
_____
_____
_____
_____
_____
_____
_____
_____

Today's Prayer

_____
_____
_____
_____
_____

对罪的知觉

Day 29

My Conscience Awakened

Surely I was sinful at birth, sinful from
the time my mother conceived me.
—Psalm 51:5

Wake-up time was 5:30 a.m. We quickly got cleaned up and converted our living room and sleeping area into a prayer room. For the next two and a half hours, we, the unbelievers, prayed as we were guided by the evangelist. Then we began our first meeting, where instruction on the Bible was given. Beginning with Genesis, the story of humanity was unfolded to us.

Afterward came breakfast, and then we went back for another three-hour meeting, when the human condition was expounded to us. This was the first time I was confronted with my sinfulness. I always thought myself a pretty good person. I had never spent a night in jail, had never been arrested, and had never committed any crimes. They focused the teaching meeting not on external crimes and sins but on the internal state of our hearts and souls.

Even now, I can recall vividly the moment my conscience was awakened. The evangelist drew out a scenario of the final judgment of God, in which God would open the books and call my name: "Sarah Liu, come forward!" Terror possessed me as I pictured that moment.

The evangelist said that no one could hide from God and that the thoughts of my heart would be exposed. The evangelist went on to say that if I were to deny that I was a sinner, the books would record the exact moment of all my sins, in such-and-such year, month, day, and, yes, it even would record the instances of my sinful thought. Then God would conclude with having me removed from His glorious presence and thrown into the lake of fire that never ends!

Back when I pondered suicide, I had convinced myself that to die was to end my suffering. Now I learned that to die was to account for my miserable life. This was more than I could bear! It was all so vividly before me. All that night, I tossed and turned in anguish over my sin. How could I possibly escape such a day from coming?

Who would save me from such horror? —

What Do You Think?

What are your first memories of recognizing your own sin? How aware were you of coming judgment?

Today's Reflection

_____
_____
_____
_____
_____
_____
_____
_____
_____
_____
_____
_____
_____
_____
_____
_____
_____
_____

Today's Prayer

_____
_____
_____
_____
_____
_____

降服于耶稣

I Surrendered All

Praise be to the Lord, for he showed his wonderful
love to me when I was in a besieged city.
—Psalm 31:21

The second day began like the first— prayer, Bible
study, breakfast, and more Bible studies. Though
the routine was similar, the message was not. That
day's message was the answer to my heart's cry in
the night, "Who will save me from such horror?"

The evangelist, a young lady, spoke to us about
Jesus, beginning with His birth and why He left
heaven to be with us. With every word she spoke,
the message became more and more marvelous.
Could this really be?

Then she, in the most vivid language, began to
describe His suffering and death ... for me. I could
see in my mind's eye His beatings and torture; the
crown of thorns upon His brow; forced to carry His
own cross; nailed to the cross and lifted high for all
to see. Why? Why would He do all this? To satisfy

God's justice that I, Sarah Liu, could be saved from my sin and the judgment to come.

This knowledge was too wonderful for me. The message that day exceeded the sorrow of my sin. Jesus, the Savior of the world, at that very moment, became the Savior to Sarah Liu. I bowed, face down to the ground, and out gushed an uncontrollable flood of tears and groans. I was completely humbled by His great love for me, that He should suffer the cross in my place. This love broke down every resistance, and I surrendered all that I was.

Seized by overwhelming joy and peace, I rose up a new person. Everything was new to me at that instant—the people around me, my environment—and even the sky was brighter. I encountered my relatives outside, and they immediately perceived the change that had come over me. We all rejoiced together with a joy unspeakable and full of glory! Thanks be to Jesus Christ for His marvelous salvation. Worthy is the Lamb that was slain. Holy is His name. —

What Do You Think?

How would you describe the initial moments you understood the depth of God's love for you?

Today's Reflection

_____

_____

_____

_____

_____

_____

_____

_____

_____

_____

_____

_____

_____

_____

_____

_____

Today's Prayer

_____

_____

_____

_____

_____

CPSIA information can be obtained at www.ICGtesting.com
Printed in the USA
BVOW05s0828230414

351360BV00001B/2/P